Copyright@Cathie Wright-Lewis
All Rights Reserved
This book is the work of fiction. Names, characters, places and incidents are either part of the author's imagination, or, if real, used fictitiously.

No part of this book may be reproduced or transmitted in any form or by any electronic or mechanical means, including photocopying, recording or by any informations storage and retrieval system, without the express written permission of the publisher, except when permitted by law.

Published by Cathie Wright-Lewis
Illustrations and Cover Art by Cheyenne Angel Lewis
Information availiable at: www.cathiewrightlewis.com
ISBN-13: 978-1726422871

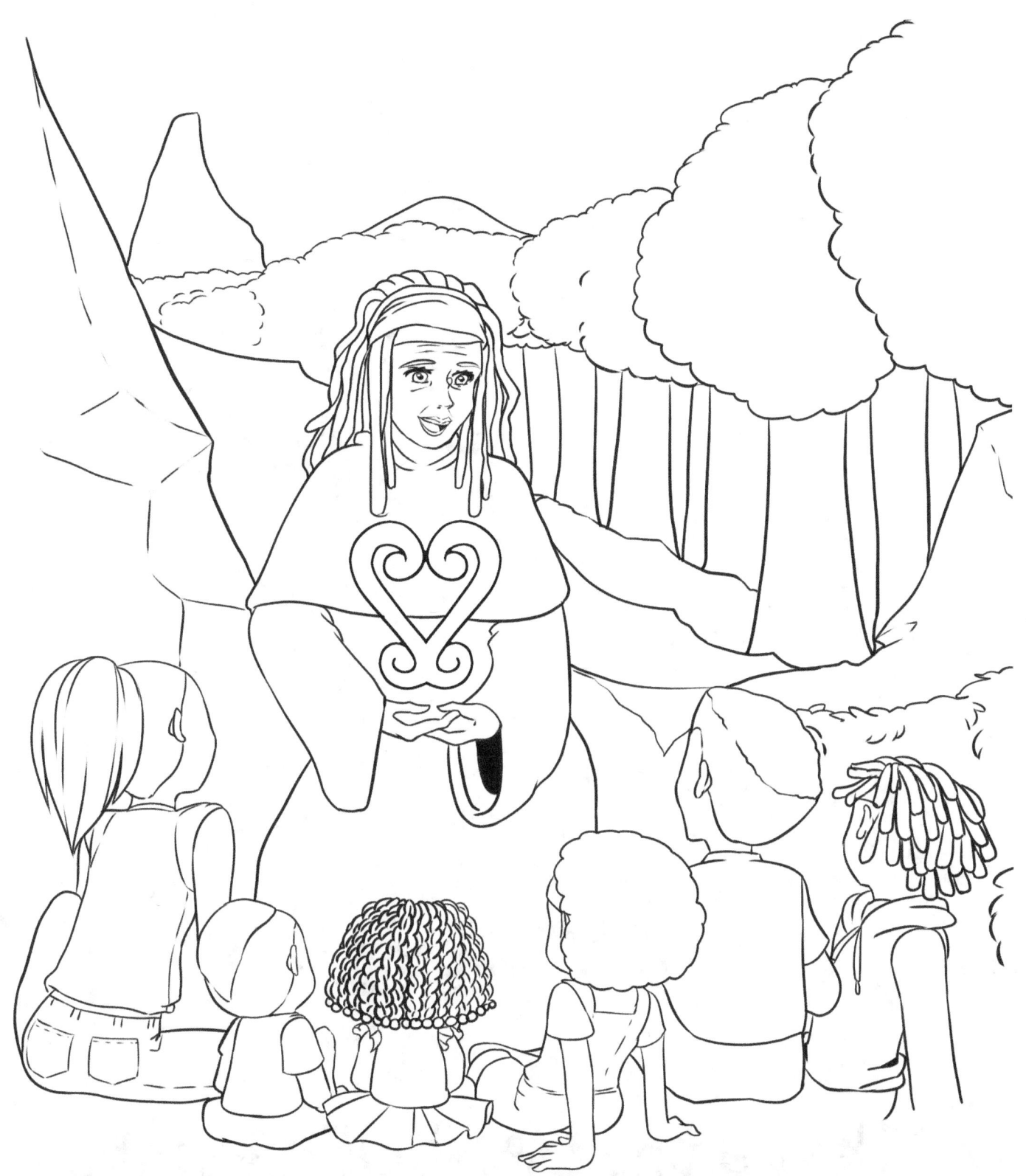

"Which one of my beautiful kinfolk remembers the meaning of this symbol?"

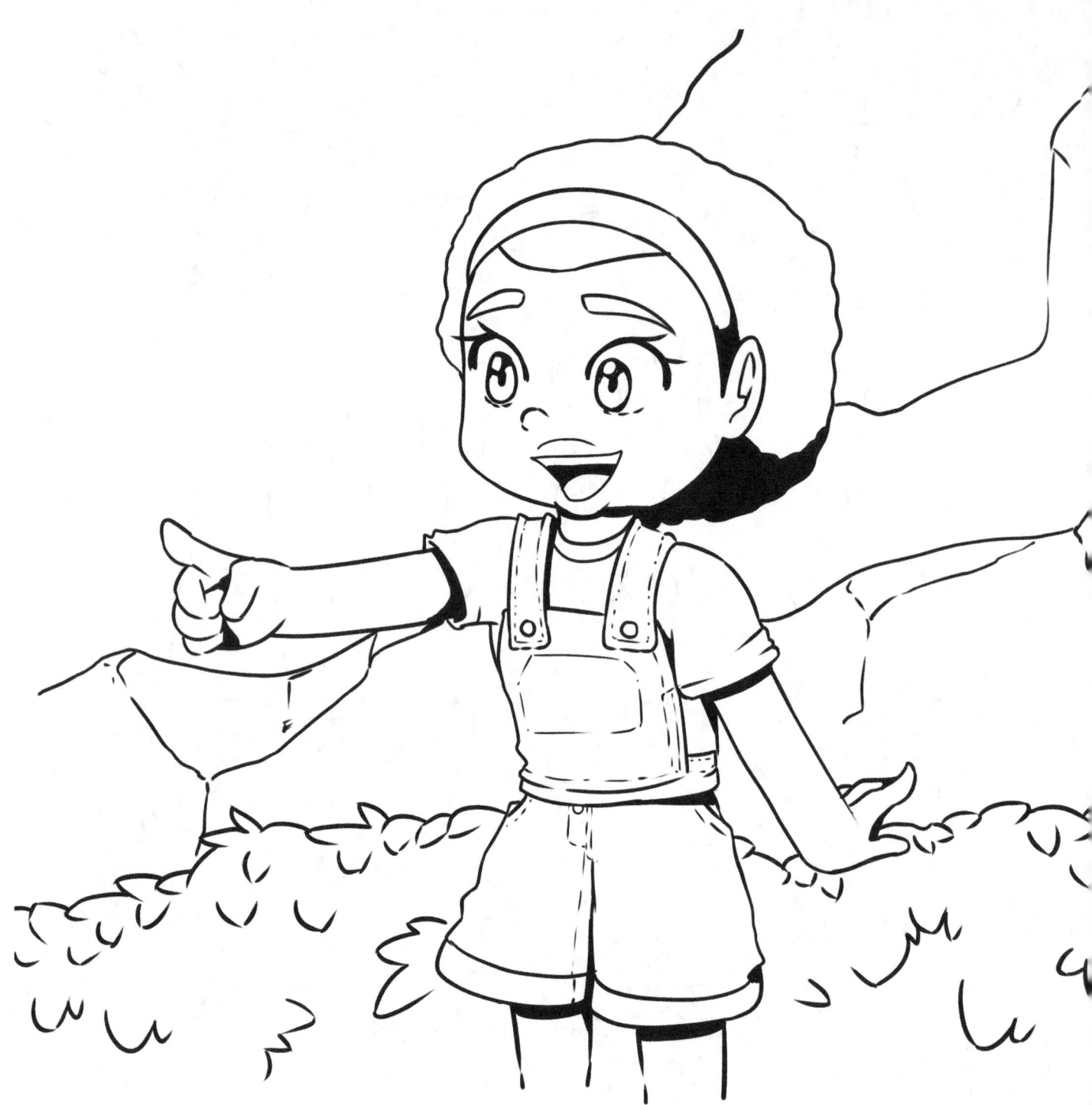

"That's the SANKOFA symbol!
It means 'to go back and fetch it'!"

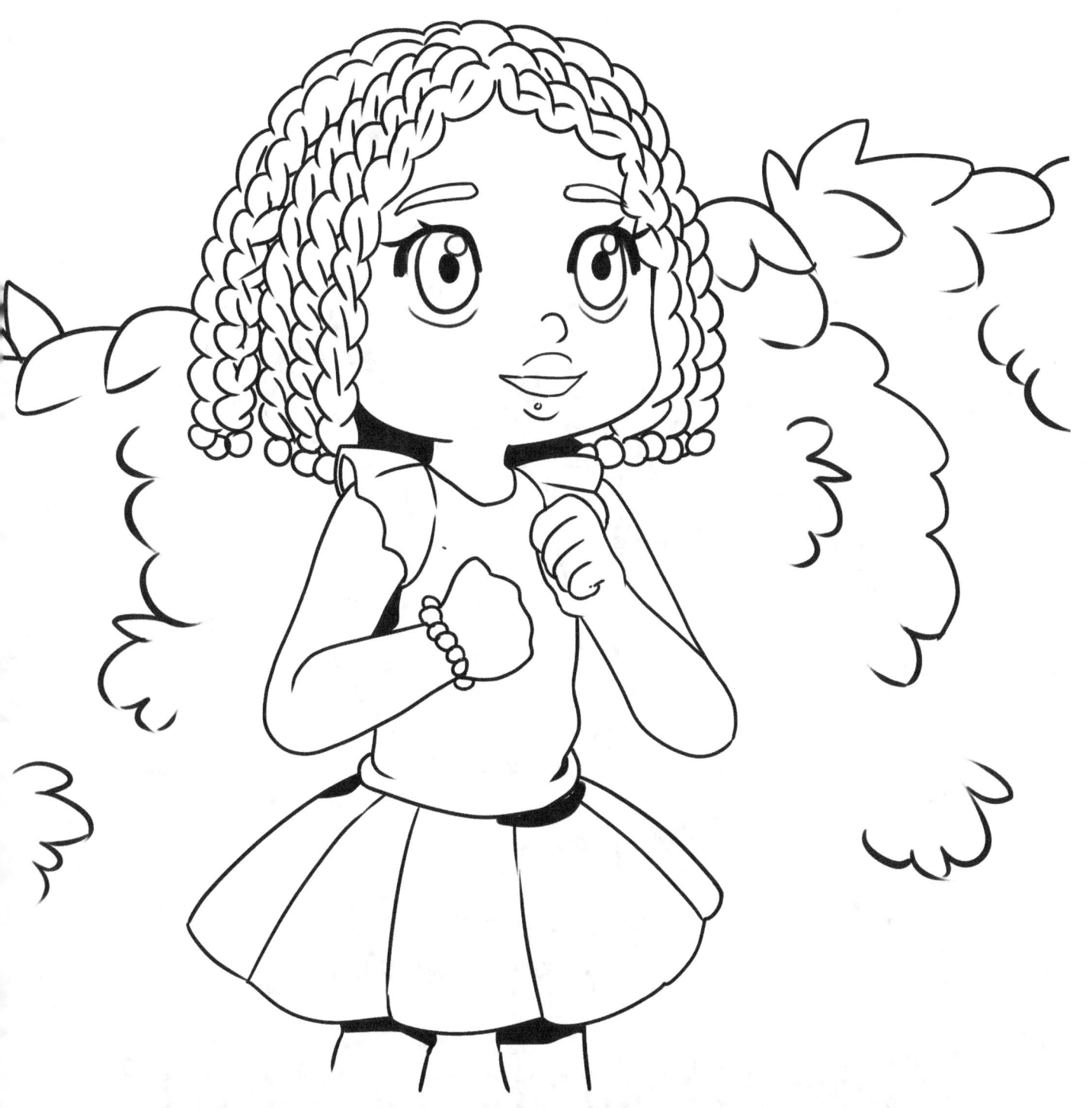

"It means we shouldn't forget our past or what it taught us."

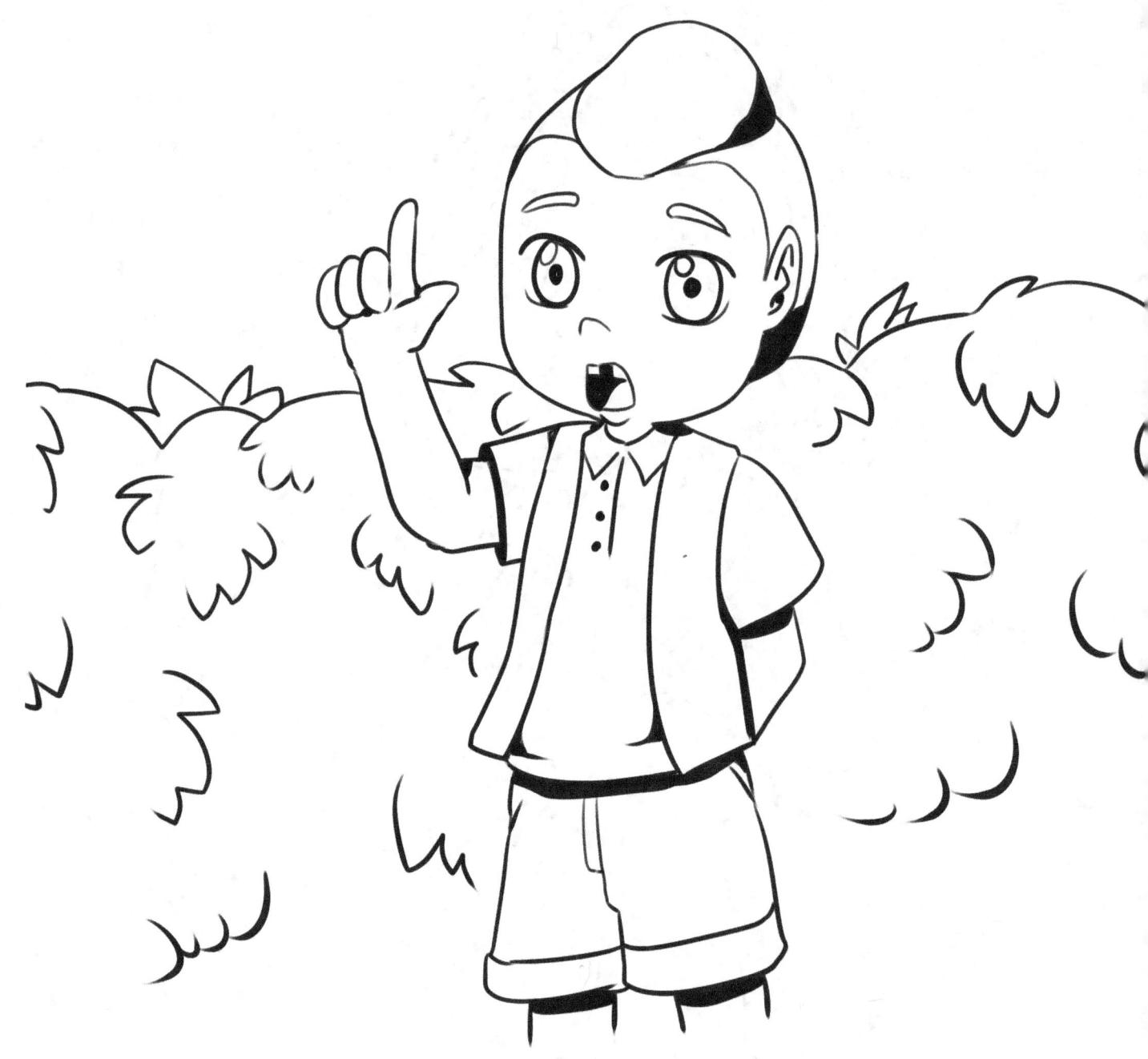

"Like fighting for rights and not sitting on the back of the bus."

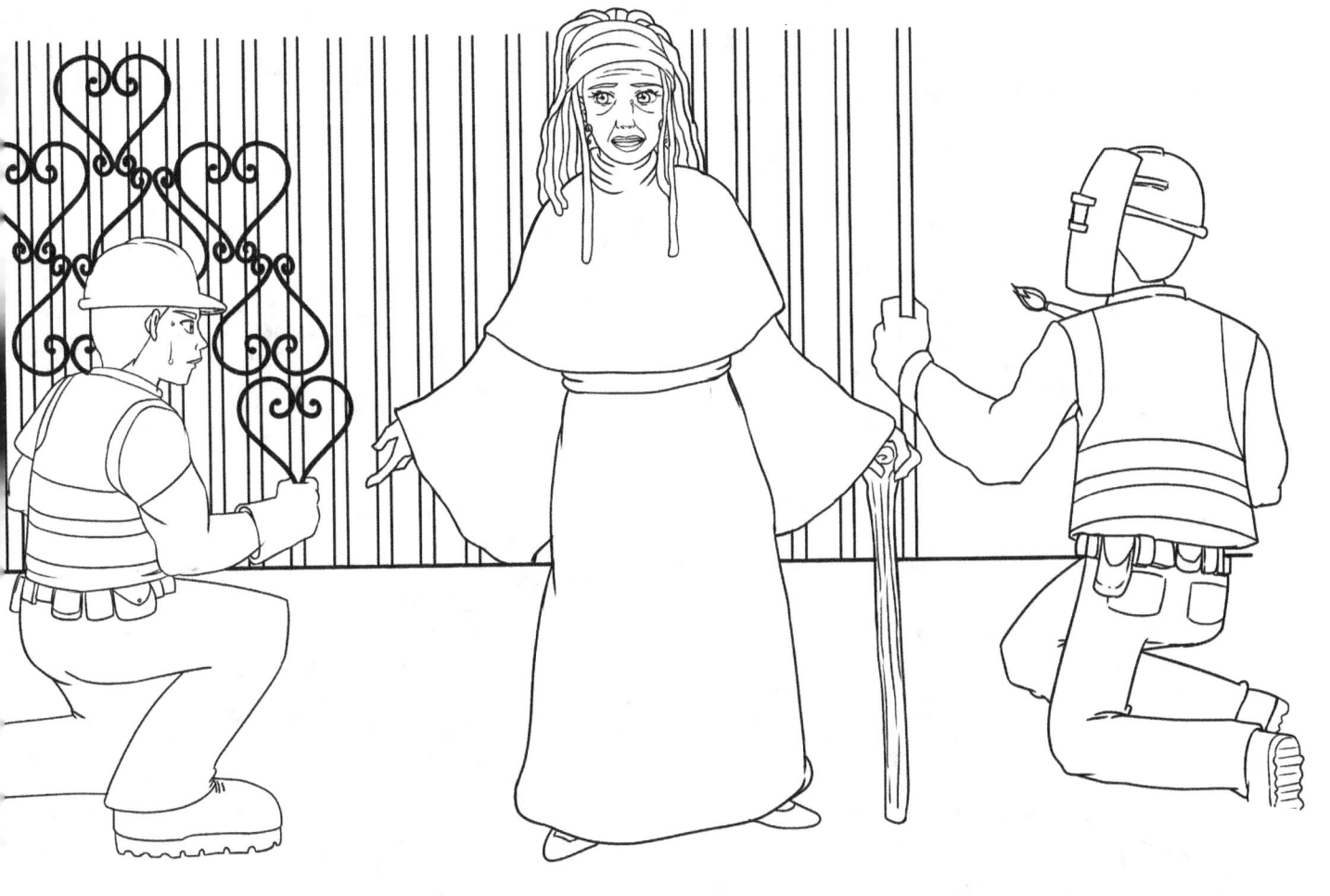

"Children, how many have seen these kind of gates before?"

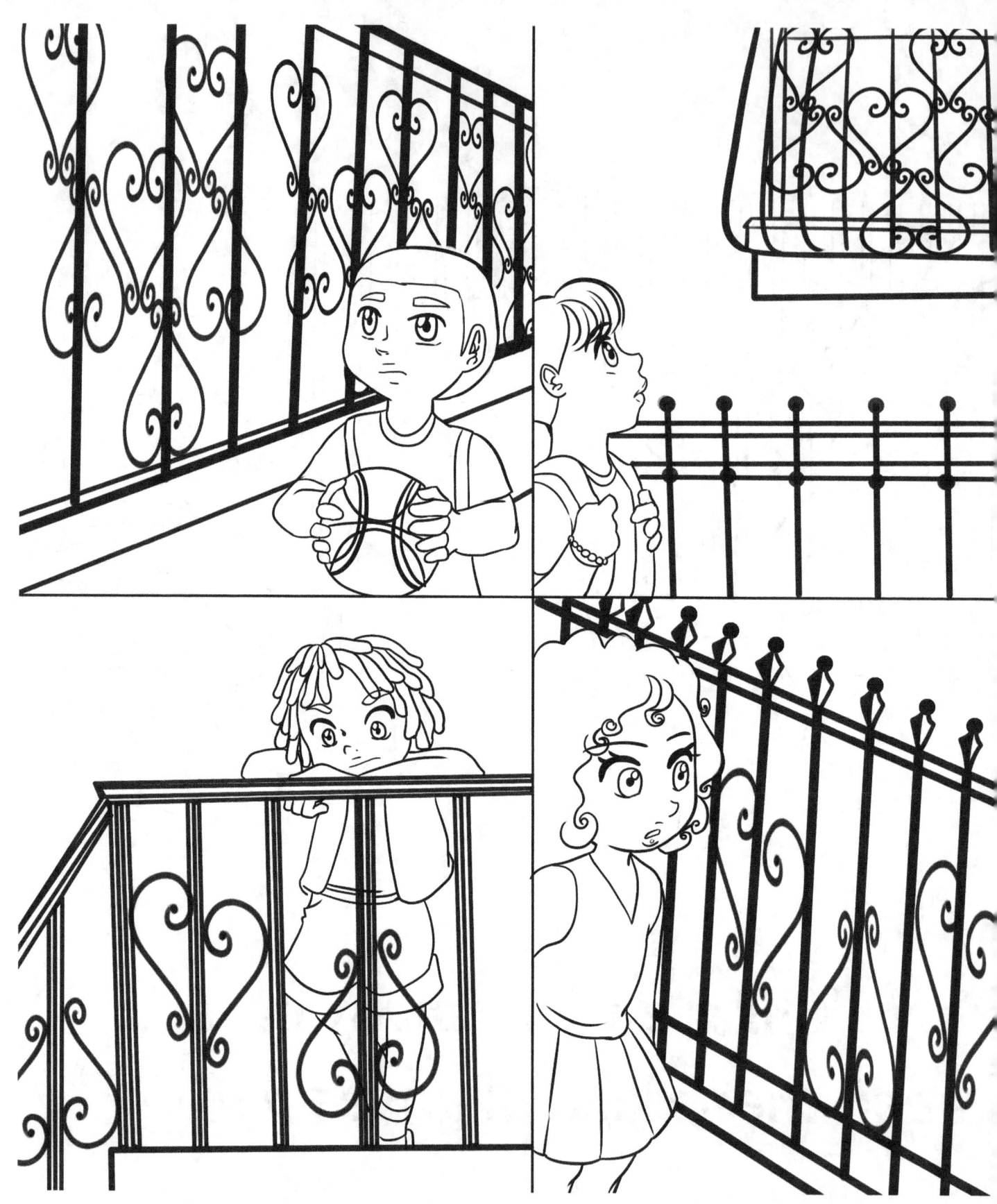

"It's on the gate outside our door."

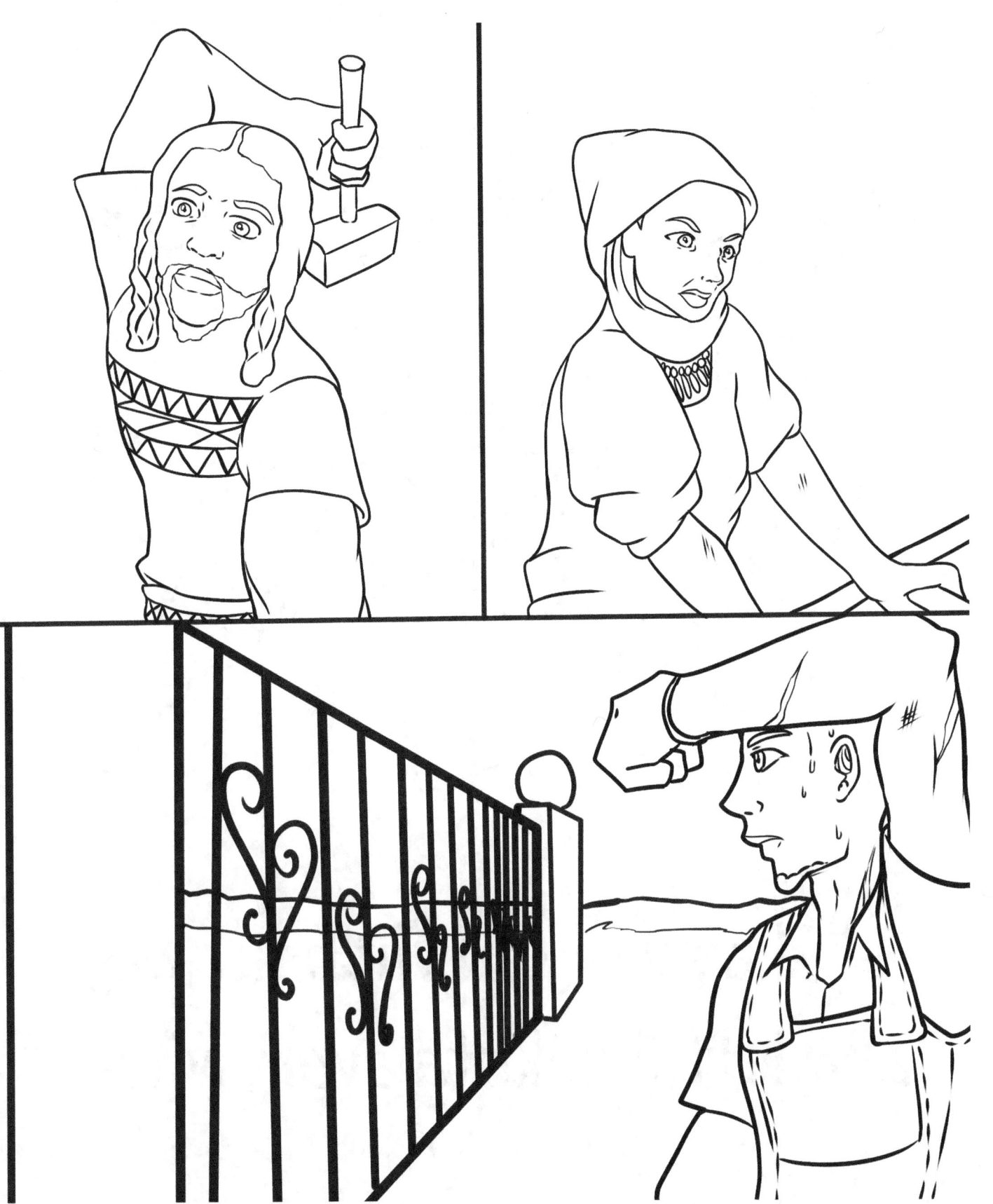

"Our ancestors left Sankofa so we would never forget they were here."

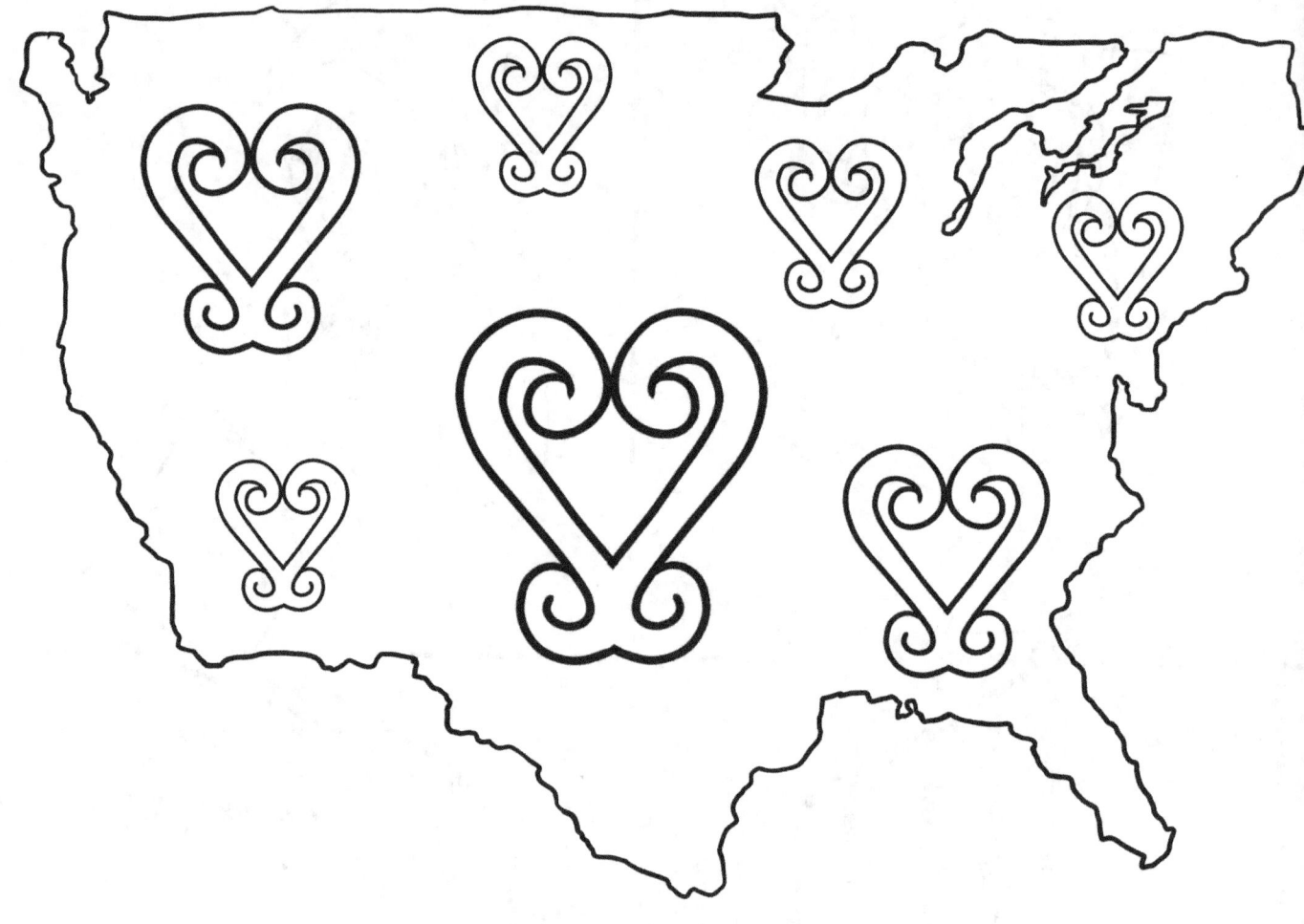

"They worked without pay and left Sankofa everywhere."

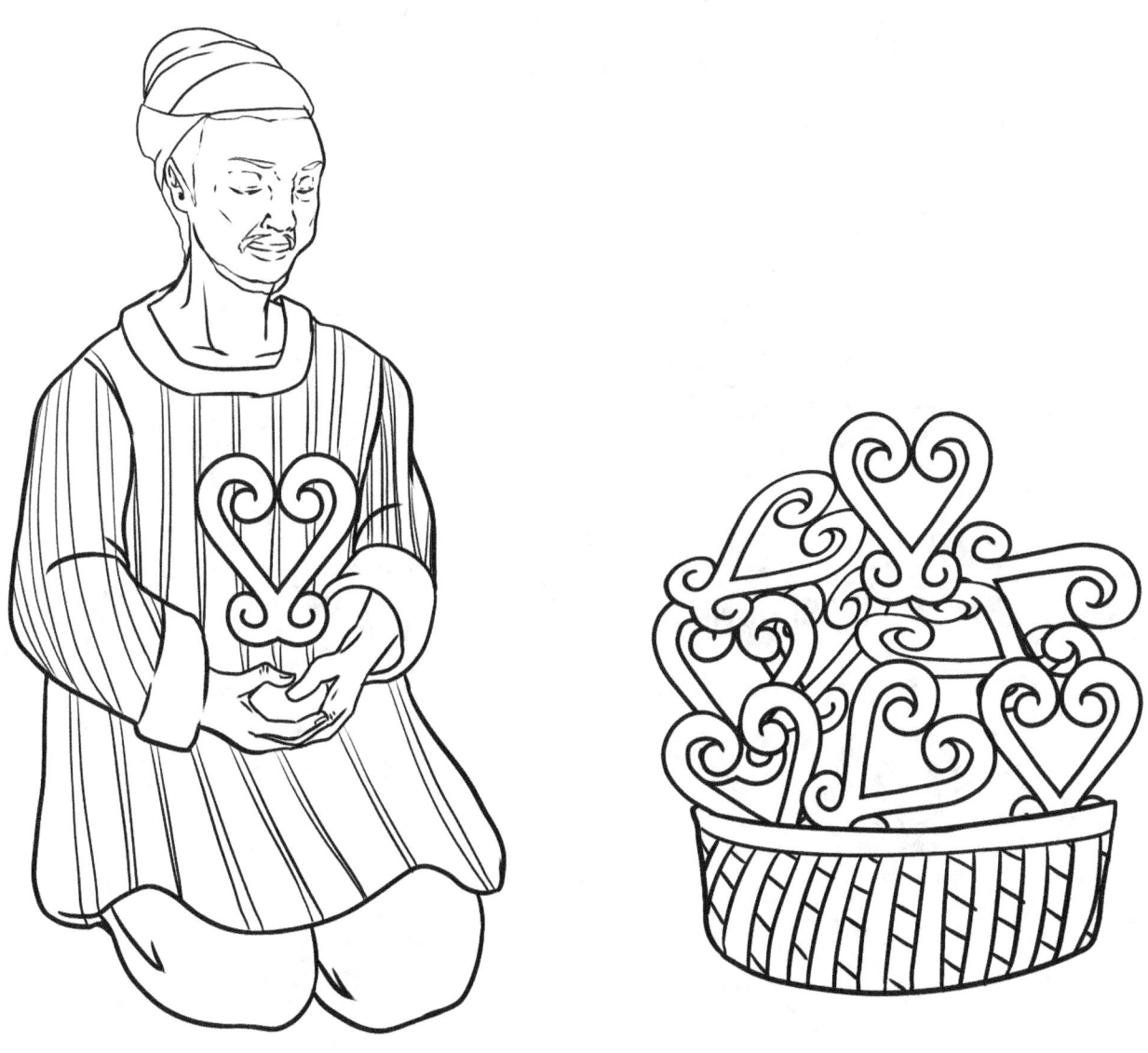

"Sankofa is the proof for all to see."

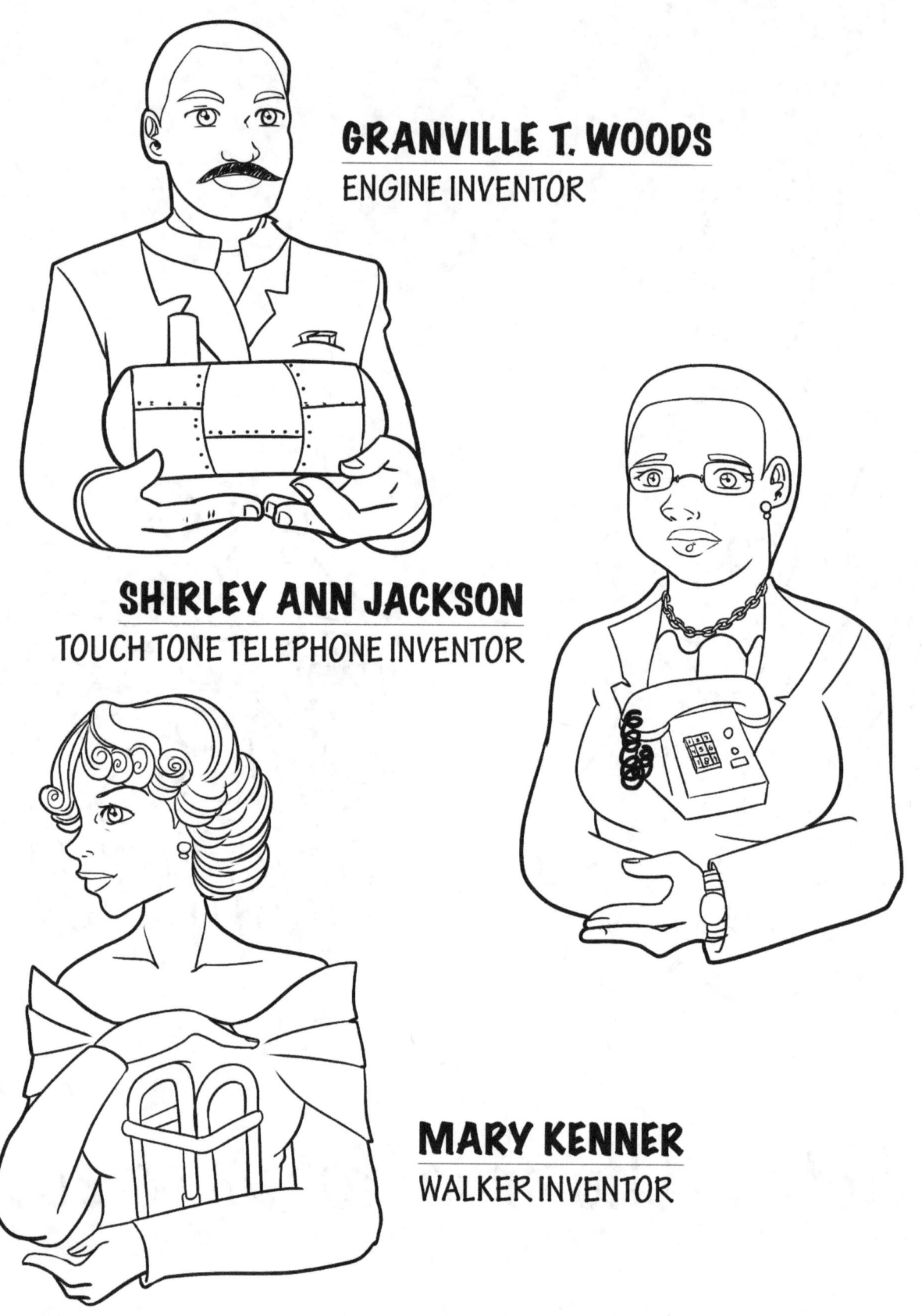

GRANVILLE T. WOODS
ENGINE INVENTOR

SHIRLEY ANN JACKSON
TOUCH TONE TELEPHONE INVENTOR

MARY KENNER
WALKER INVENTOR

"Without our African ancestors...

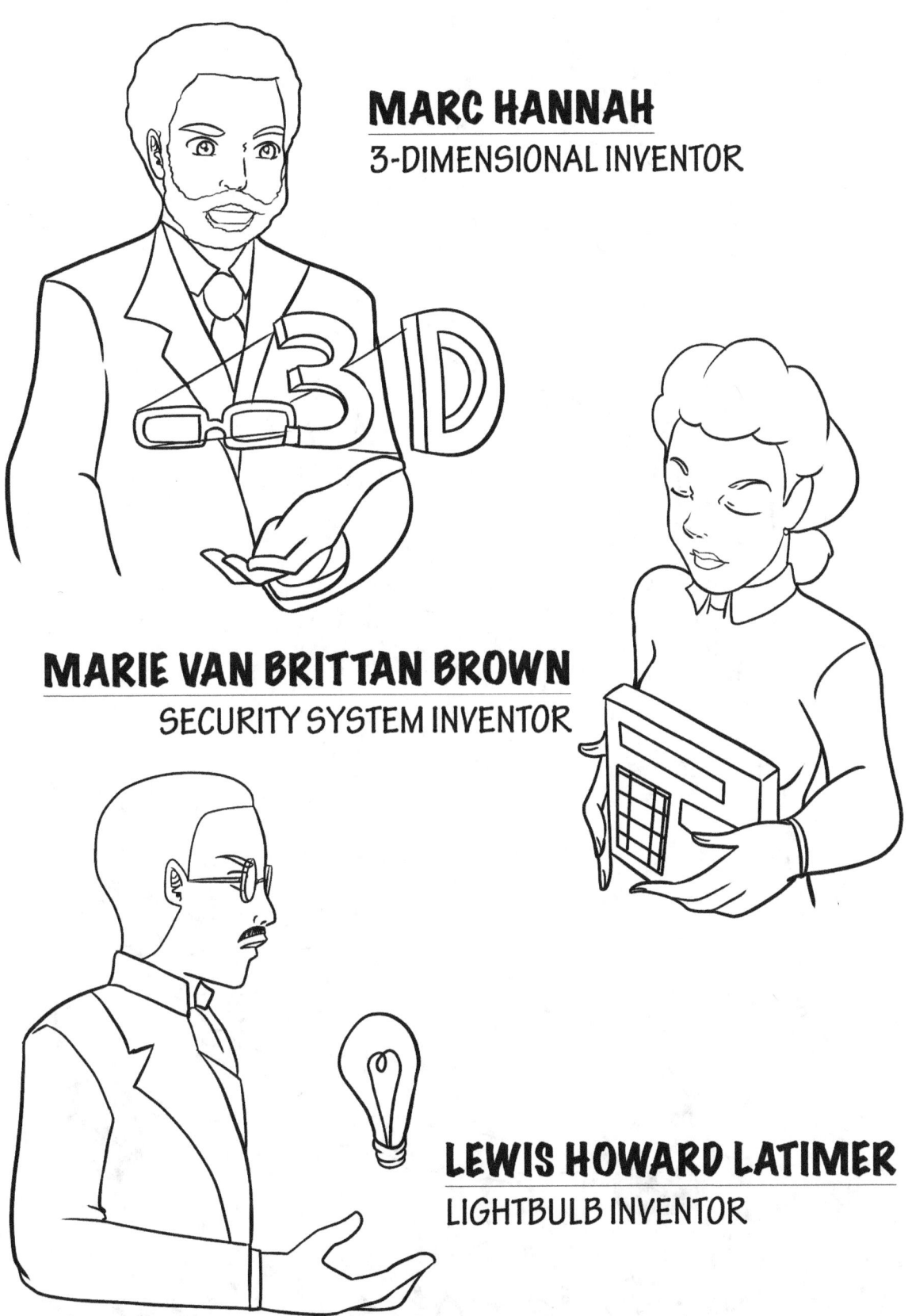

MARC HANNAH
3-DIMENSIONAL INVENTOR

MARIE VAN BRITTAN BROWN
SECURITY SYSTEM INVENTOR

LEWIS HOWARD LATIMER
LIGHTBULB INVENTOR

... America would never be."

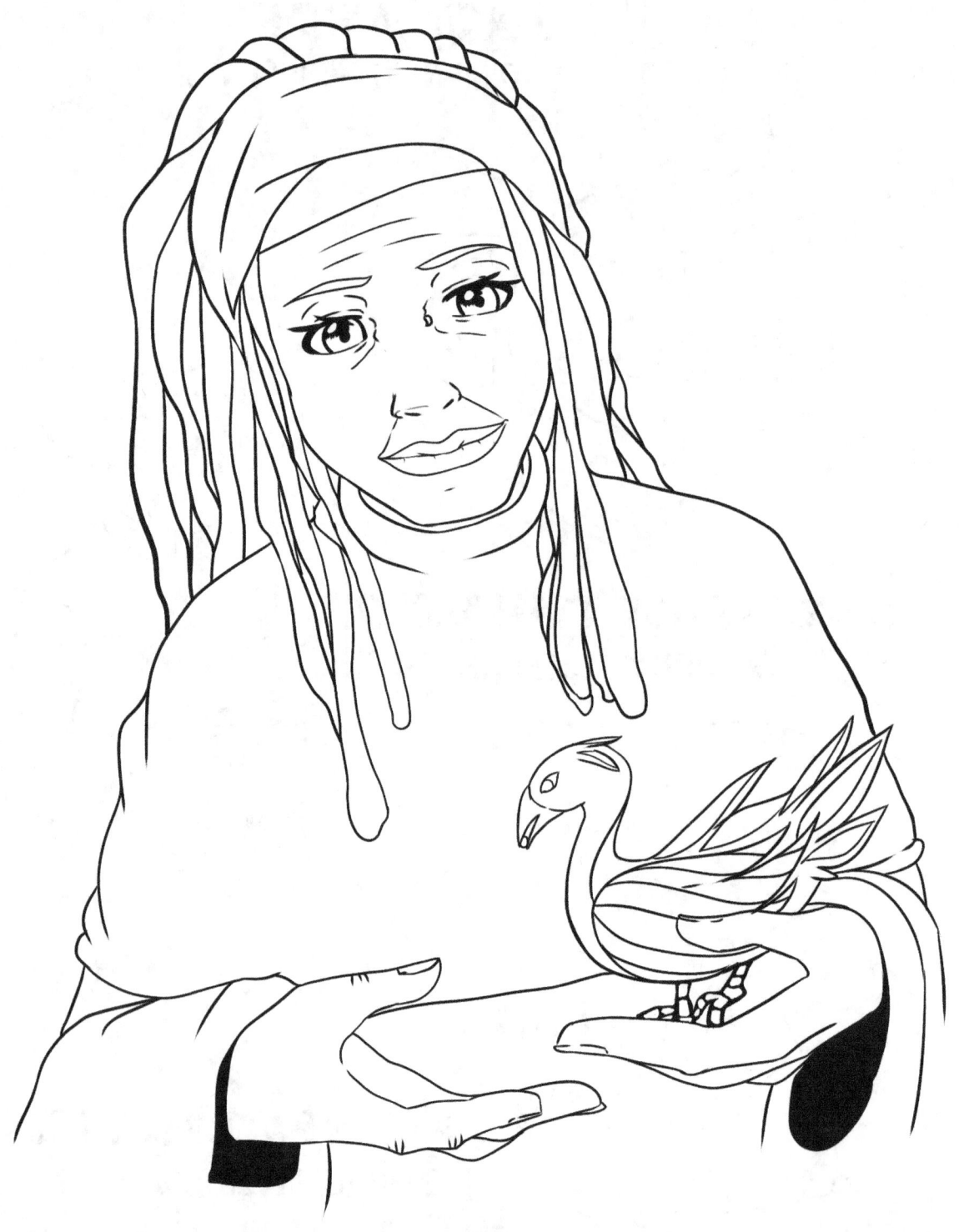

"Sankofa is not only hearts. There's a Sankofa bird, in fact."

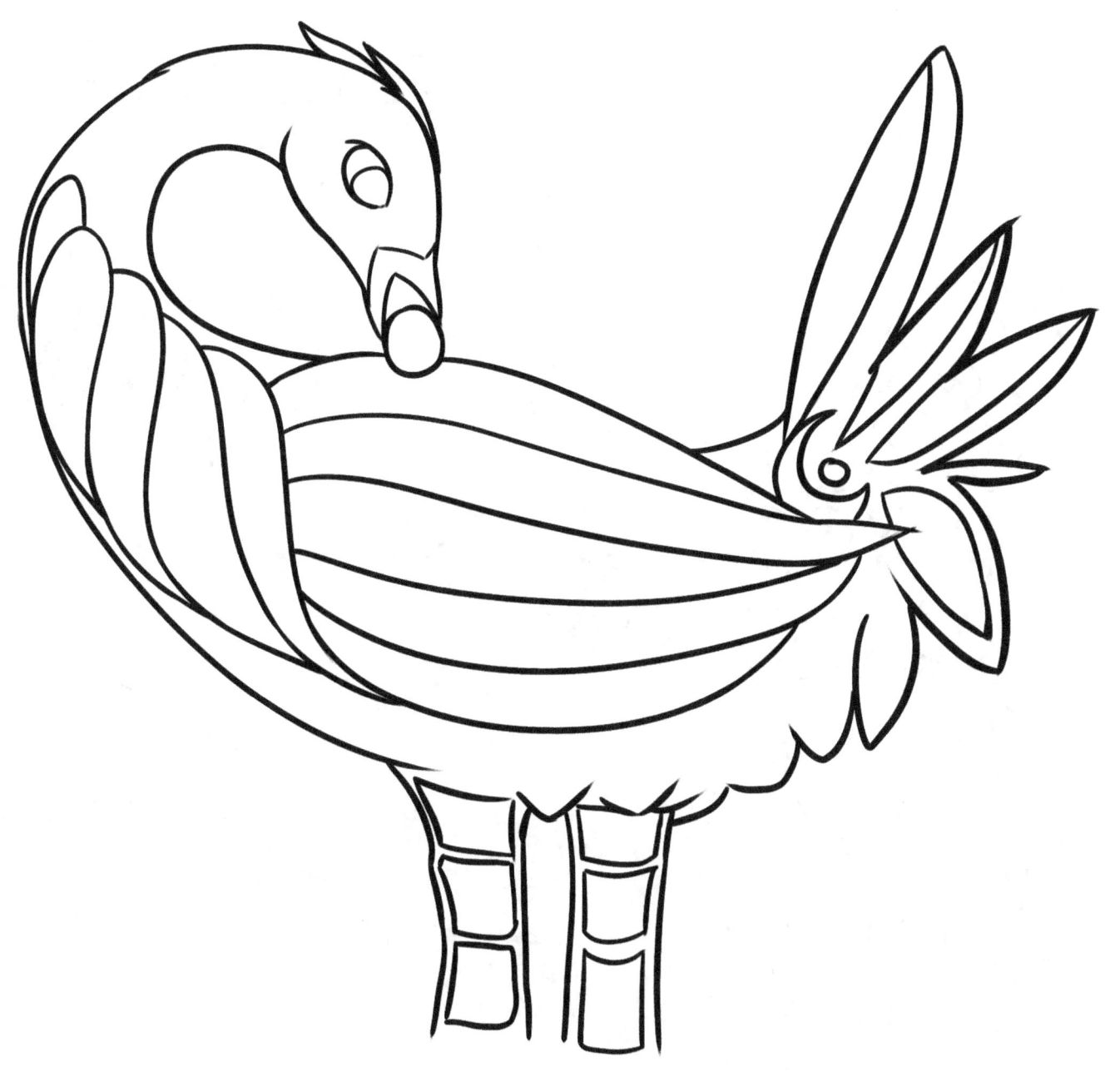

"Its head turns backwards taking an egg off its back."

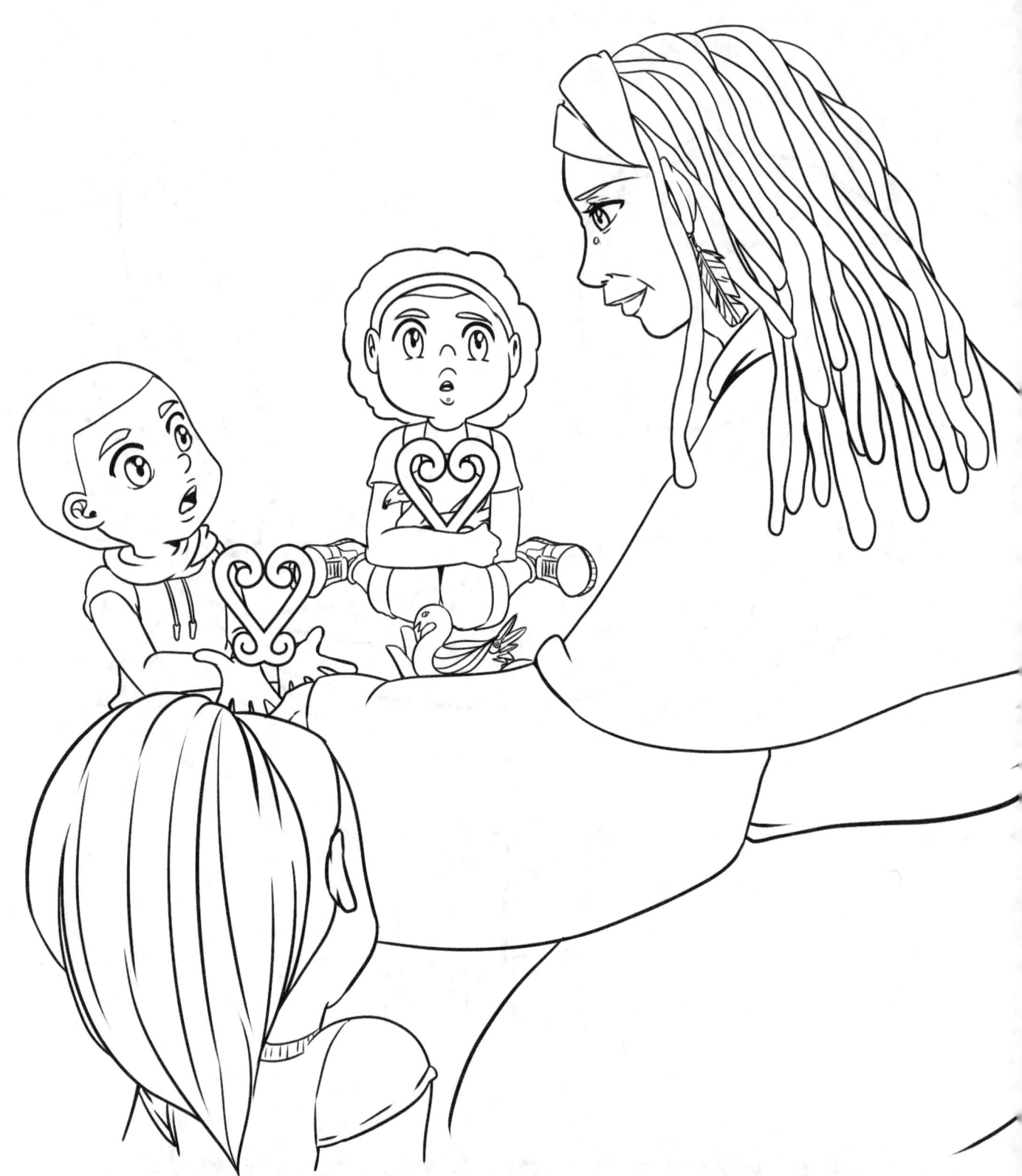

"The bird and the heart both mean the same."

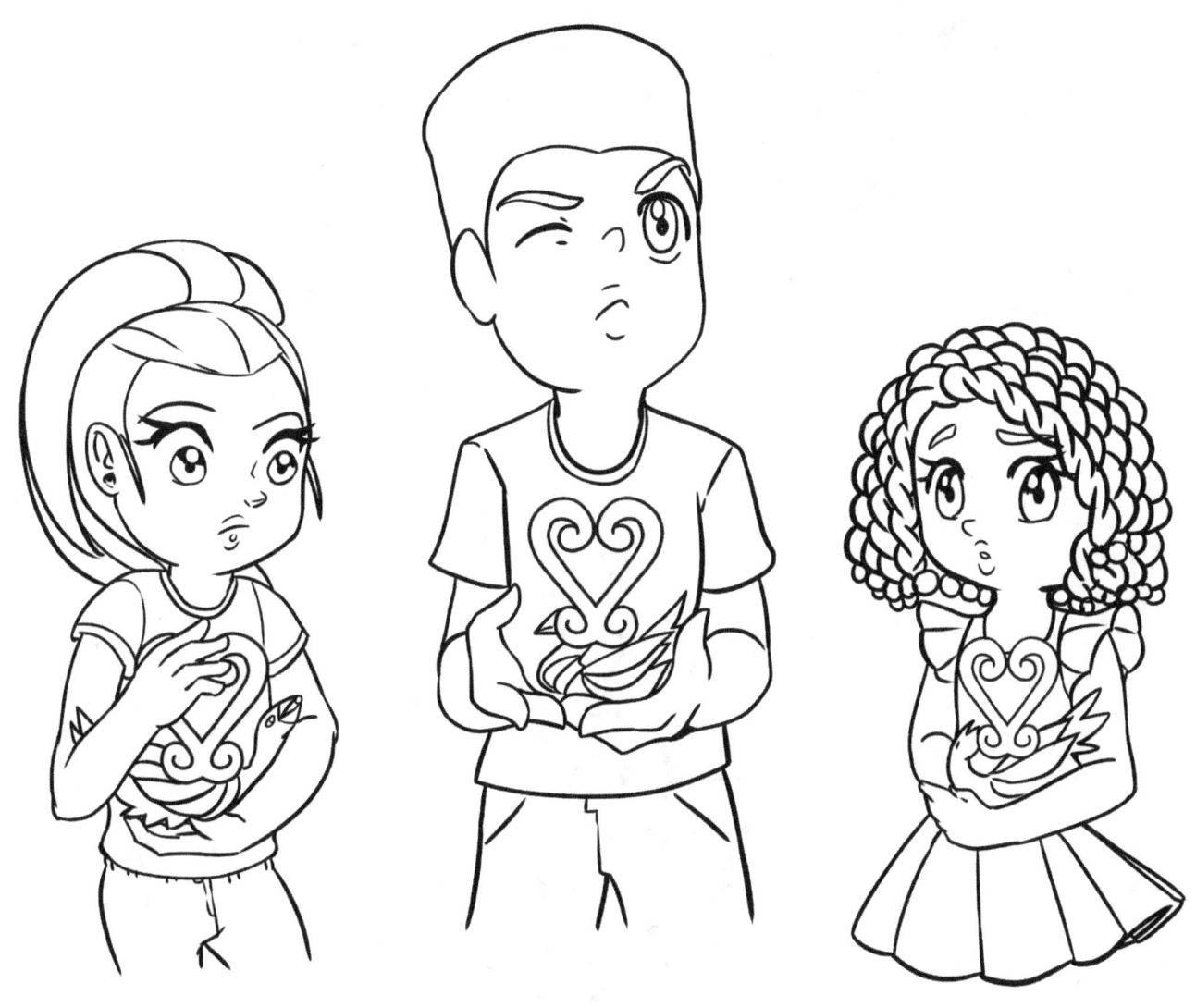

"Go back and fetch your history, your culture, your name."

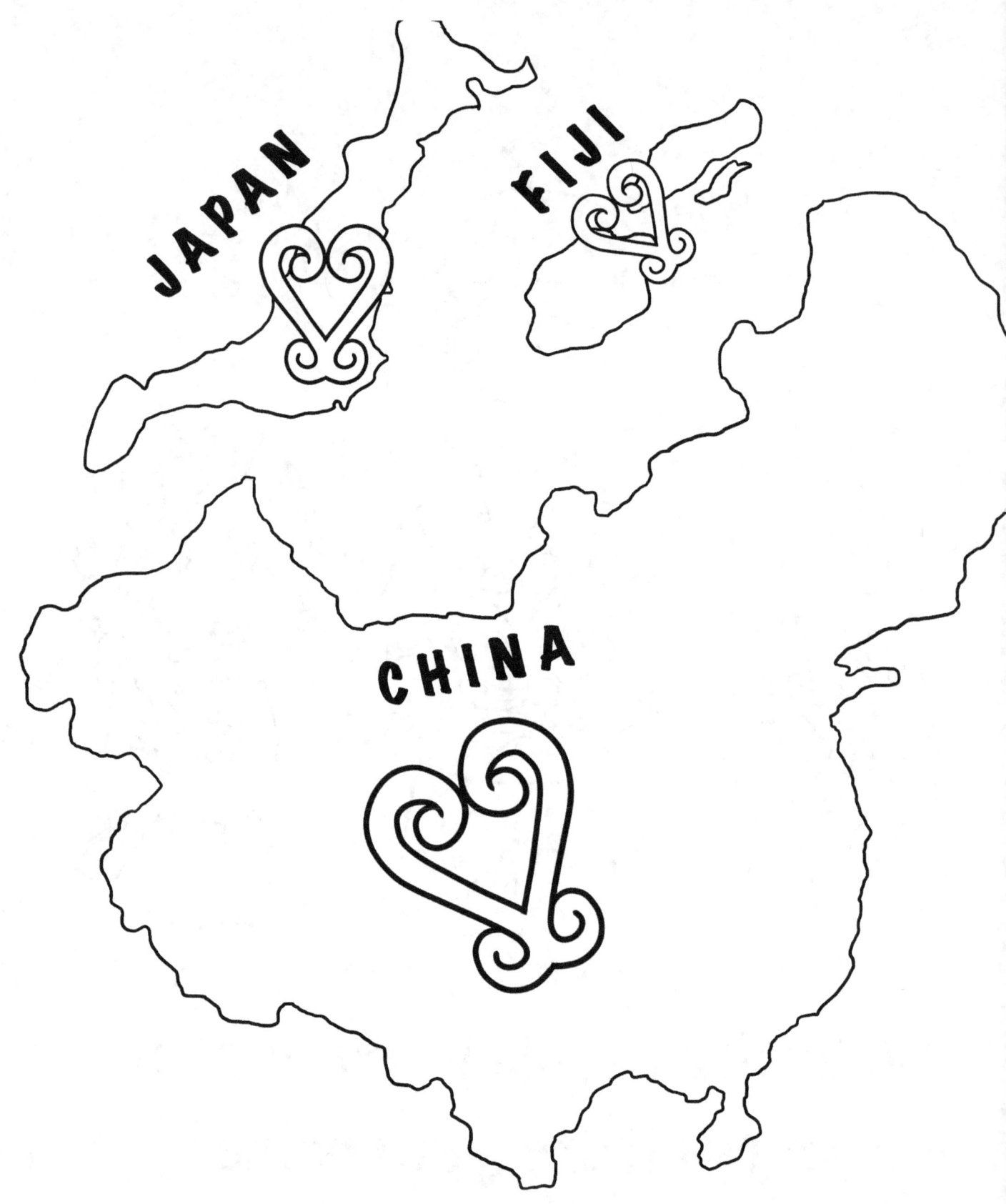

"Our ancestors left Sankofa in places like Japan, China, Australia...

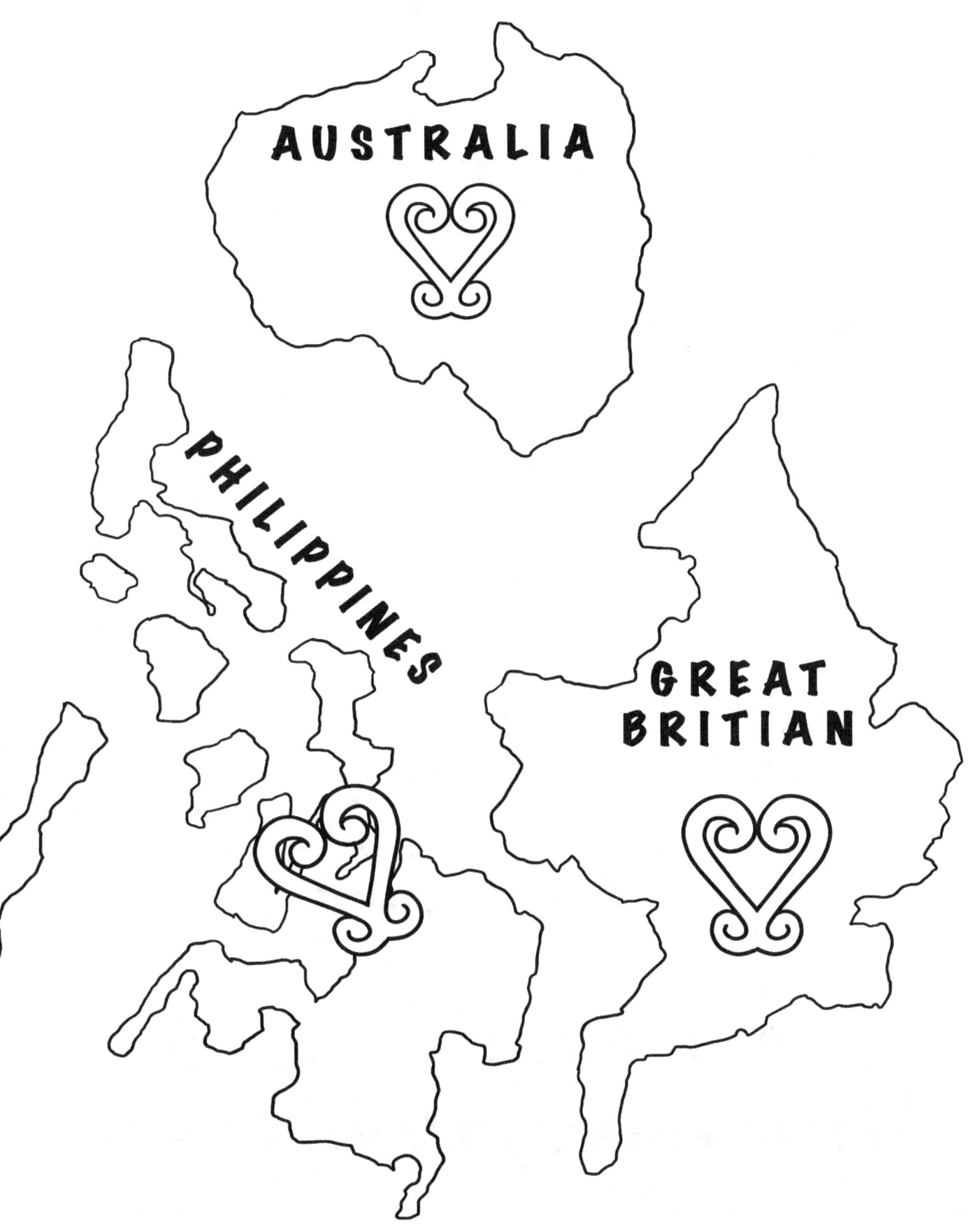
...South America and even Fiji."

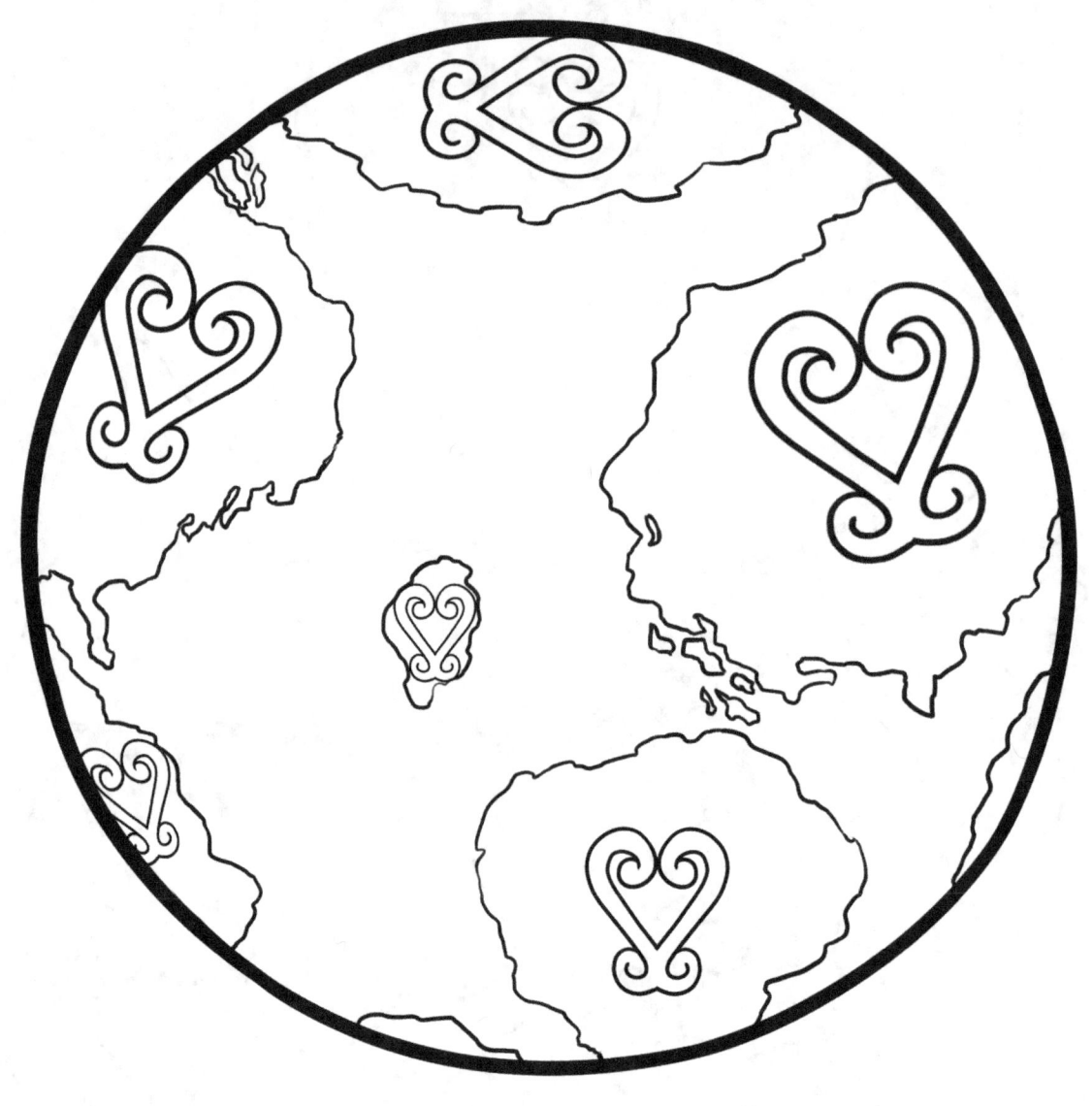

"African Ancestors were explorers long before slavery."

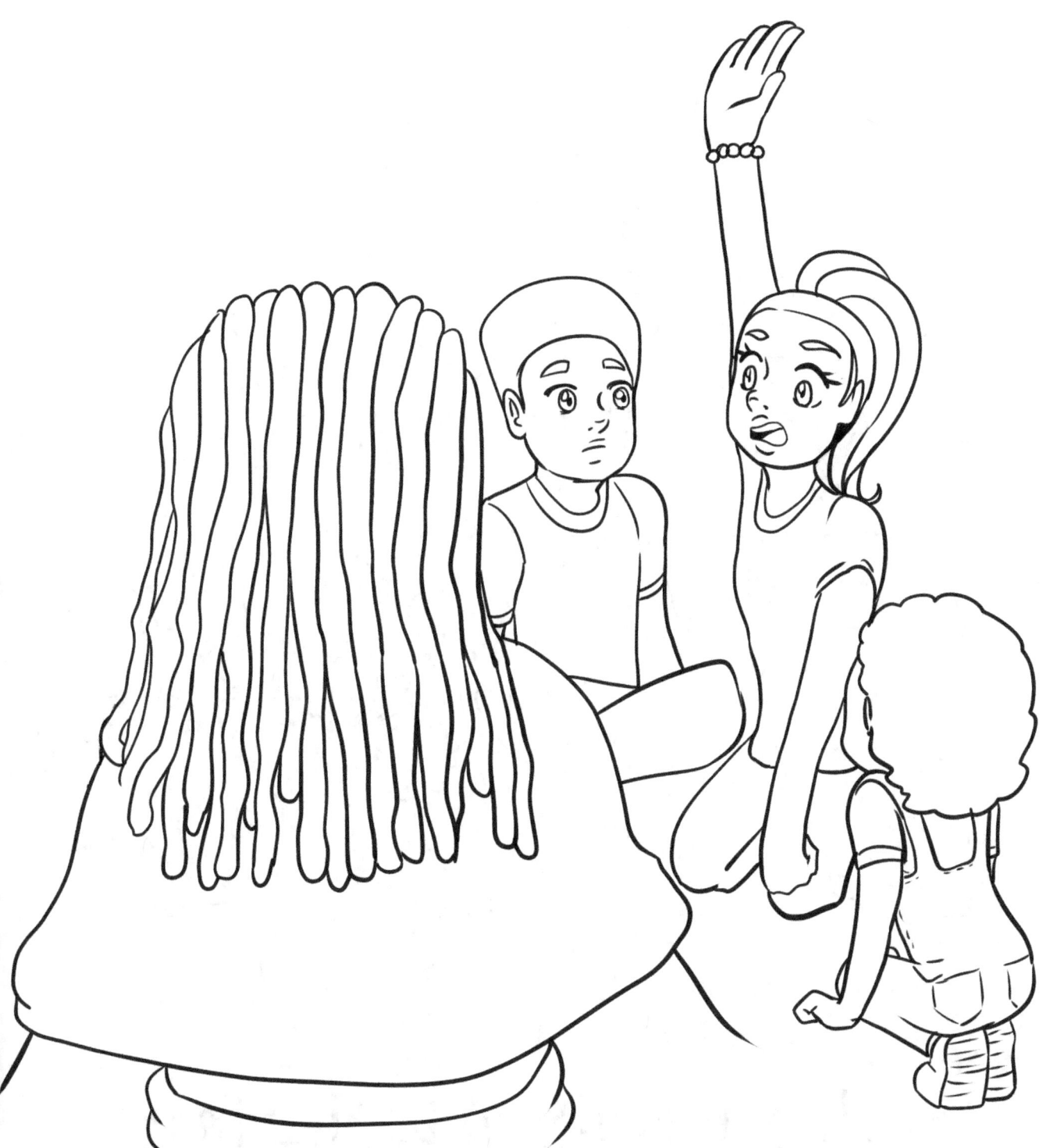

"Mama Relly, what are we to fetch?
What do our ancestors want us to do?"

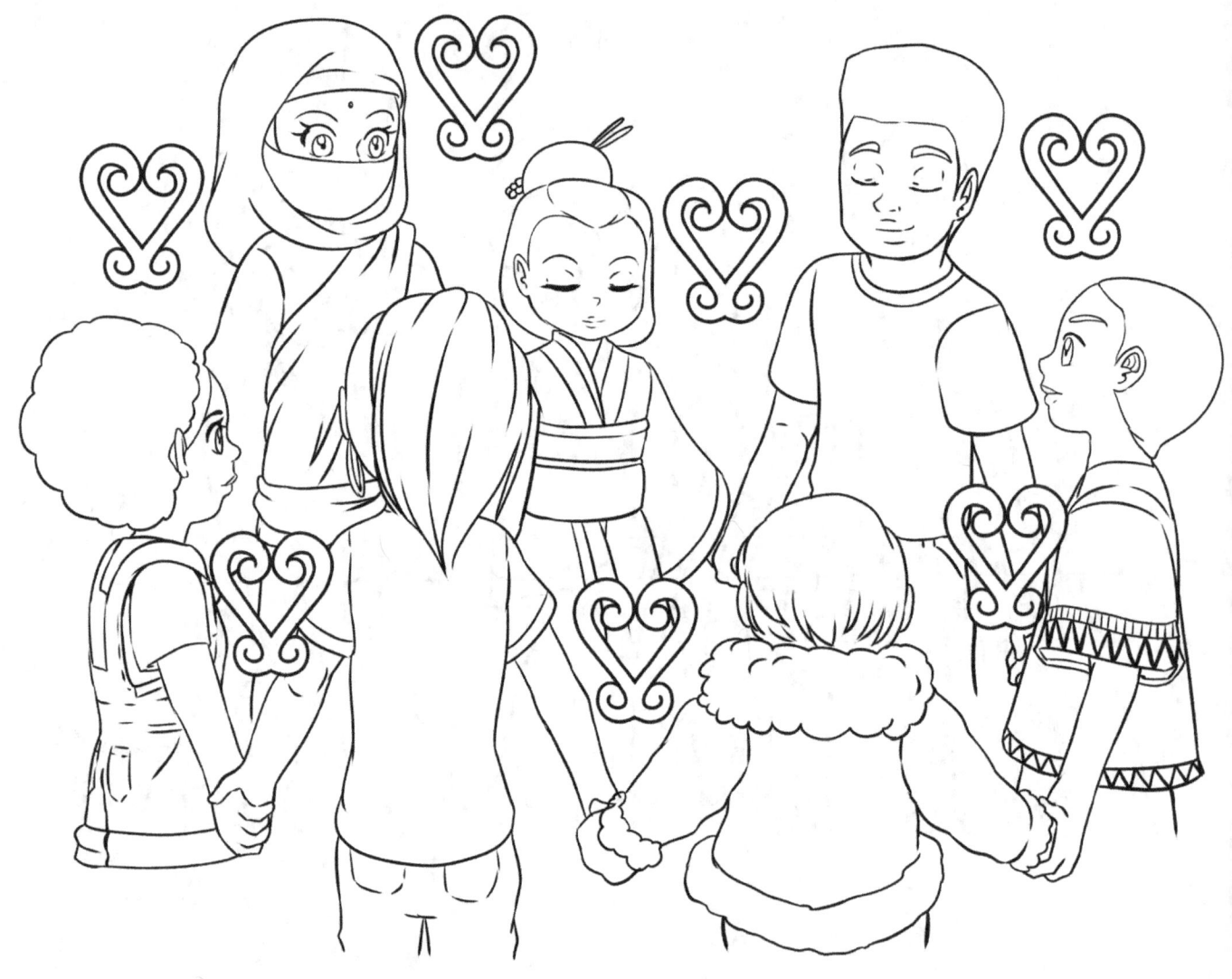

"They want you to live in a world of peace where everyone remembers what is true."

"Never forget Sankofa."

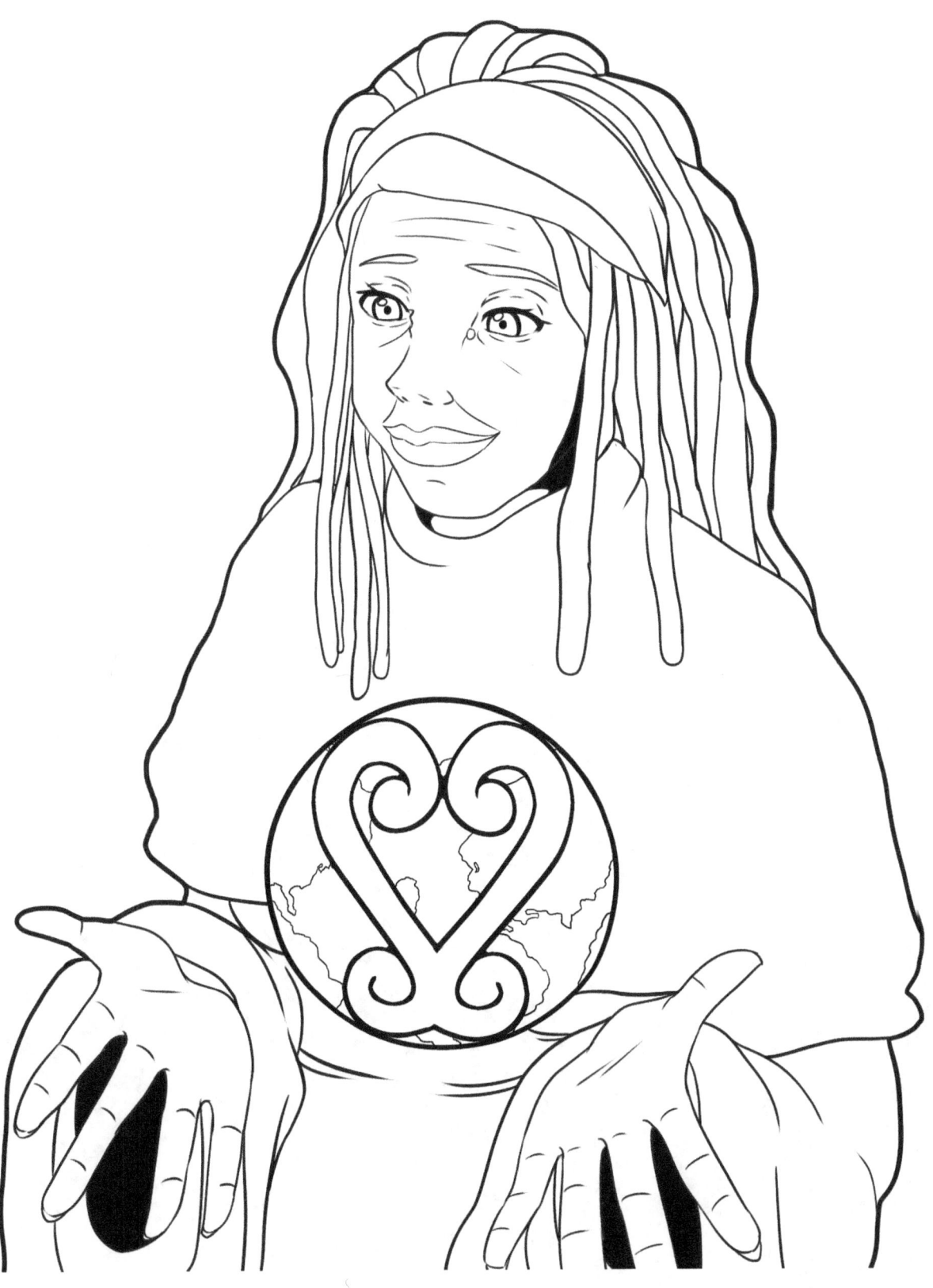